Who Split the Atom?

Who Split the Atom?

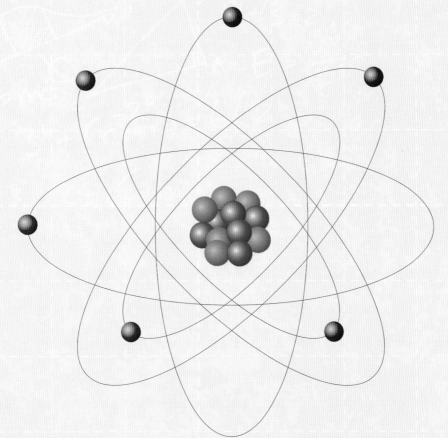

Anna Claybourne

ARCTURUS

This edition first published in 2010 by Arcturus Publishing
Distributed by Black Rabbit Books
P.O. Box 3263
Mankato, Minnesota 56002

Printed in China

Planned and produced by Discovery Books Ltd.
www.discoverybooks.net
Managing editor: Laura Durman
Editors: Amy Bauman and Penny Worms
Designer: Ian Winton
Illustrator: Stefan Chabluk

Library of Congress Cataloging-in-Publication Data

Claybourne, Anna.
  Who split the atom? / Anna Claybourne.
      p. cm. – (Breakthroughs in science and technology)
  Includes index.
  Summary: "Looking at some of the major inventions and discoveries shaping our world today, Breakthroughs in Science profiles the research leading up to the discovery (not just profiles of the one or two key "players"). Each book describes the "famous" moment and then examines the continued evolution illustrating its impact today and for the future"– Provided by publisher.
  ISBN 978-1-84837-683-0 (lib. bdg.)
 1. Atoms–Juvenile literature. 2. Matter–Constitution–Juvenile literature. 3. Discoveries in science–Juvenile literature. I. Title.
  QC173.16.C535 2011
  539–dc22
                                 2010011015

Picture Credits
Corbis: cover (Martial Trezzini/EPA) 9 (Bettmann), 12 (Bettmann), 26 (DK Limited), 35 (Bettmann), 36, 40 (Martial Trezzini/EPA), 42 (Steffen Kugler/EPA). Getty images: 11 (William Fetter Douglas/The Bridgeman Art Library), 31 (Hulton Archive), 32 (Central Press), 39 main (Anne-Christine Poujalat/AFP). iStockphoto.com: 24 (Thomas Bercic). Library of Congress: 14 (painted by J. Lonsdale Esq; engraved by C. Turner, ARA), 28. NASA: 34. Science Photo Library: 17 (Charles D Winters), 18 (Science Source), 41 (CERN), 43 (Equinox Graphics). Shutterstock: 6 (Rafael Ramirez Lee), 15 (Jip Fens), 38 (Craig Hanson), 39 top (Albert Lozano). Wikimedia Commmons: 10 (Johann Kerseboom), 13 (Jacques-Louis David).

SL001449US   Supplier 03, Date 0510

Contents

What is an atom?

Building blocks

All the objects you can see and feel around you—your chair, this book, your clothes, and even you yourself—are made of billions of tiny **atoms**. Atoms are the building blocks of **matter**. They are what stuff—all stuff—is made of.

As you know, there are different types of matter, from wood to water, paper to plastic, stone to steel. All these things are made of different types of atoms—either on their own or in combination with other atoms.

All the objects and people you see around you are made up of billions and billions of tiny atoms. The atoms join together in different patterns to make molecules, which make up millions of substances.

What is matter?

Matter is all the materials and objects and substances around us, including solids, liquids, and gases. Not everything is matter—for example, light and sound are forms of **energy**. However, as scientists have discovered, matter and energy are closely related, and one can be turned into the other.

There are only around 100 types of atoms, which make basic substances known as **elements**. For example, gold, oxygen, and iron are elements, each made of just one type of atom. But combined with each other, the basic atoms make the millions of different substances and materials we see all around us.

Atoms and molecules

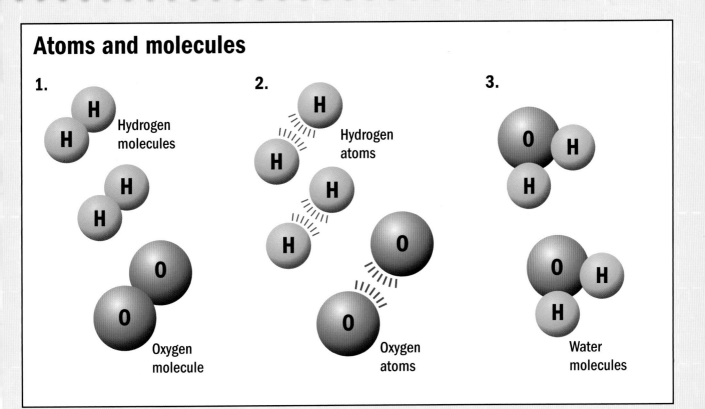

1. Hydrogen molecules

Oxygen molecule

2. Hydrogen atoms

Oxygen atoms

3. Water molecules

How small?

Atoms are really, really tiny. You cannot see individual atoms with the naked eye. They are so small that 100 million atoms, all lined up in a row, would only reach across your little fingernail.

Splitting the atom

It took many years to discover and understand atoms. At first, people believed that atoms were the smallest unit of all, and that something so tiny could not be split into smaller parts. But during the 20th century, scientists learned otherwise. They found that they could split atoms apart. And what they discovered led to some hugely powerful and dangerous results. In this book you'll find out how the atom was split and what it meant for all our lives.

Oxygen and hydrogen atoms join together in pairs to make molecules of pure oxygen and hydrogen (1). They can also split apart (2) and join with other atoms. One oxygen atom joined to two hydrogen atoms makes a water molecule (3).

THAT'S A FACT!

When you look at or touch any object, you're seeing or feeling billions of atoms packed together. For example, a page in this book is about one million atoms thick, and one glass of fruit juice contains about 25 trillion trillion (25,000,000,000,000,000,000,000,000) atoms!

The ancient atomists

The idea that everything is made up of tiny units has been around since ancient times. The name *atom* comes from an ancient Greek word, *atomos*, which means "uncuttable or indivisible." The word was first used by two ancient Greeks, Leucippus and his follower Democritus, who lived around 2,400 years ago. They used it to describe little invisible units that they believed everything was made of. They also correctly thought that there were different kinds of atoms of varying sizes, which made up every kind of material. People who agreed with this theory were known as the "atomists." Ancient Indian **Buddhist** thinkers around a thousand years later had similar ideas, known as Buddhist atomism.

> "*Nothing exists except atoms and empty space; everything else is just opinion.*"
> Democritus declares his view of reality.

However, that long ago, there was no way of really looking at atoms, and Leucippus and Democritus had no good evidence for their idea. They simply thought it seemed like a sensible explanation. It happened to be along the right lines, according to what we know today—but this was only proved in the last 200 years.

Democritus is such an important figure in Greek history that he was featured on the 100 drachma bank note. The drachma currency was replaced by Euros in Greece in 2002.

According to ancient Greek religion, the sun was a god, Helios, riding his chariot across the sky. But Democritus realized the sun was a star, like all the other stars in the sky.

THAT'S A FACT!

Atoms weren't the only thing that Democritus was uncannily right about. He studied many subjects and came up with all sorts of ideas. He claimed that the earth was round, the sun was a star like the other stars but closer, and that early people didn't have language but developed it gradually. Scientists today have found evidence that proves all these things to be true.

Greek philosophers

Many ancient Greek **philosophers** spent a lot of time wondering about how the world worked. While some suggested everything was made up of atoms, others thought everything was essentially made of water, or from different types of air. While they didn't always guess correctly, this way of asking questions and coming up with ideas was very important. It paved the way for modern scientific thought and methods.

Breakthrough

More than 2,000 years ago, the ancient Greek atomists, Leucippus and Democritus, came up with the first theory of atoms, and how they make up all substances. Their ideas were not widely adopted, but they would be revived much later.

Understanding matter

The four elements

Despite the atomists' theories, most ancient philosophers thought that instead of many types of atoms, there were just four basic substances, or "elements": earth, fire, air, and water. The idea of these four elements carried on for many centuries, into **medieval** and **Renaissance** times. However, in the 1600s, a new age of detailed scientific study was born and people began to question the "four elements."

A new approach

Scientists did careful experiments, mixing, combining, and breaking down different types of substances to see what they were really made of. It became clear that there had to be more than just four ingredients making up the universe.

Brilliant Boyle

One of the most important scientists of the time was Irish experimenter Robert Boyle. He argued that matter was made of atoms after all, and that there were many different types of basic atoms and elements, not just four. He wrote a book called *The Sceptical Chymist*, published in 1661, explaining that atoms moved around and joined together in groups to make different substances.

Robert Boyle

Date of birth: January 25, 1627

Place of birth: Lismore, Ireland

Greatest achievement: Boyle revolutionized the science of matter, turning it from superstitious alchemy into modern, evidence-based chemistry.

Interesting fact: Boyle was also interested in anatomy and finding out how the bodies of animals and humans worked—but he couldn't bear to dissect bodies as it made him feel ill.

Date of death: December 31, 1691

Alchemy

Boyle's work grew out of alchemy, an ancient practice of trying to treat or change everyday substances, such as lead and stone, to create more valuable substances, such as gold. It didn't work, but it did involve a lot of experimentation and resulted in some useful discoveries.

Boyle said that scientists should do proper, careful experiments to find clear evidence of what matter was made of and how it worked. This was really the beginning of the modern science of chemistry—the study of substances and how they behave, join, break apart, and change. Boyle studied many things, including how gases behave under pressure and how freezing and burning worked.

Thanks to Boyle, old myths were replaced with proper experiments and evidence, and the idea of four elements was swept away. The search began for the real elements—the many different types of atoms.

This 19th-century painting by William Fettes Douglas shows an alchemist at work. You can see his chemical-mixing equipment and a potion he is concocting.

Breakthrough

Robert Boyle's book, *The Sceptical Chymist* (1661), and his experiments marked a new direction in the study of the science of matter.

Atoms and elements

Amazing discoveries

Boyle's breakthrough ideas influenced many other scientists. Through the 1700s, they devised lots of experiments to find out more and more about matter. They especially wanted to discover the different types of atoms that existed, and the elements, or basic substances, that they made.

In experiments to make metals **react** with acids, British chemist Henry Cavendish released the element hydrogen. He studied this new gas and found that it was lighter than air and burned easily. He went on to prove that hydrogen and oxygen reacted together to make water; so water was definitely not a pure element. It was made of hydrogen and oxygen atoms.

Other experimenters, including Joseph Black and Joseph Priestley, isolated and tested various elements, such as oxygen and carbon. They showed how the elements combined to make substances such as carbon dioxide.

The elements didn't always have the same names as they do now—for example carbon dioxide was known as "fixed air" and hydrogen "inflammable air." But that was about to change.

As hydrogen is lighter than air, it was eventually used to fill airships and make them fly. But its highly flammable qualities led to terrible disasters, such as the loss of this airship, the *Hindenburg*, in 1937.

Lavoisier

The king of chemistry was Frenchman Antoine Lavoisier. Working in the late 1700s, he discovered many elements, or types of atoms, and made a list of 33 elements that had been found so far. He came up with a naming system and gave oxygen, hydrogen, and other elements their modern names. He set out rules for **chemical reactions** and experiments, so that all chemists could follow the same practices and compare their results. He also helped to set up the metric measuring system that scientists still use today.

This picture of Antoine Lavoisier and his wife (also a chemist) shows them studying the gases that make up the earth's atmosphere.

Matter stays the same

Lavoisier defined a very important rule in chemistry: the Law of Conservation of Matter. This states that when chemicals react together and substances change, matter is never created nor destroyed—it simply changes form.

"One can assume in principle that in every operation there is an equal quantity of matter before and after the operation."
Antoine Lavoisier explains that chemical reactions neither destroy nor create matter.

Breakthrough

Antoine Lavoisier gathered together his own and other scientists' work and set out a system of rules, names, measurements, and practices for the science of chemistry. This made it easier for chemists to share and compare their work and brought chemistry into the modern age.

Dalton's atomic theory

The nature of atoms

By the beginning of the 19th century, scientists knew that there were many elements, each made of tiny atoms, which combined in different ways. But no one knew what those atoms were like because they couldn't study them closely enough. However, the more scientists found out about how elements behaved, the more they could figure out how atoms worked.

Dalton's discoveries

In 1803, a British mathematics and science teacher, John Dalton, developed a theory about atoms, which we now call the atomic theory. He did this by measuring the amounts and weights of the different elements needed to make different combinations, or **compounds**. He calculated that:

• Each element was made of one particular type of atom. For example, the element oxygen was made of only one type of atom—oxygen atoms.

• Each type of atom had a different mass (amount of matter) in it and was a different weight.

• Compounds were made when individual atoms joined together in a particular formation, called a molecule.

John Dalton

Date of birth: September 6, 1766

Place of birth: Cockermouth, England

Greatest achievement: With his atomic theory, presented in 1803, Dalton explained how atoms differ from each other and how they form molecules.

Interesting fact: Dalton was color-blind and was the first scientist to study and identify color blindness.

Date of death: July 27, 1844

Looking at carbon dioxide

You can see Dalton's theory in action if you think about a common compound, such as carbon dioxide.

Carbon atoms are bigger and have more mass than oxygen atoms. To make carbon dioxide, carbon and oxygen atoms join together to form carbon dioxide molecules, each made up of one carbon atom and two oxygen atoms.

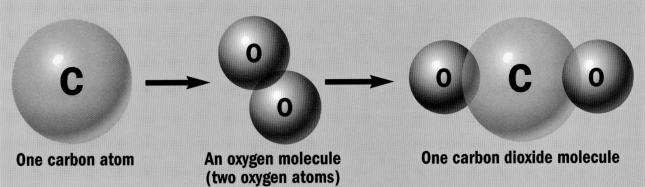

One carbon atom   **An oxygen molecule (two oxygen atoms)**   **One carbon dioxide molecule**

A molecule is the smallest possible particle of a substance. All molecules of a substance are the same, so a substance will always contain the same proportion of elements. In carbon dioxide, all the molecules have one carbon atom and two oxygen atoms, meaning carbon dioxide is the same wherever it exists.

Carbon dioxide is a common compound, usually occurring as a gas. It is used to make the bubbles in sodas and other soft drinks.

Breakthrough

Dalton's atomic theory of 1803 explained that elements were made up of only one type of atom and they each had a different mass. He described how atoms joined together in groups and patterns to make molecules. This paved the way for later scientists to find out more about atoms in detail.

Mendeleev's table

Grouping the elements

Chemistry experiments in the 1800s showed that elements could be grouped by the way they behaved. For example, some metals, such as sodium, reacted easily, even explosively, with other elements. Others, such as gold, did not react at all. Why did some elements seem to belong together in groups or families? It had to be something to do with the nature of their atoms.

A table of the elements

Since Lavoisier's time, chemists had been making lists of the elements they had discovered. In 1869, Russian chemist Dimitri Mendeleev came up with a way to organize the list of known elements into a more useful form—a table made up of rows and columns. It arranged the elements into a sequence based on the weight of their atoms and the way they behaved. This was the birth of the periodic table of elements—the ultimate list showing all the elements and their **properties** that is still used today.

THAT'S A FACT!

The elements in the periodic table have all kinds of interesting names, given to them by scientists over the years. For example, bromine comes from the Greek *bromos*, meaning "a bad smell." Helium is named after Helios, Greek god of the sun, where helium is found. Dysprosium gets its name from the Greek word *dysprositos*, meaning "hard to reach," as it was difficult to discover.

This is the modern periodic table as it looks today. It lists more than 100 known elements.

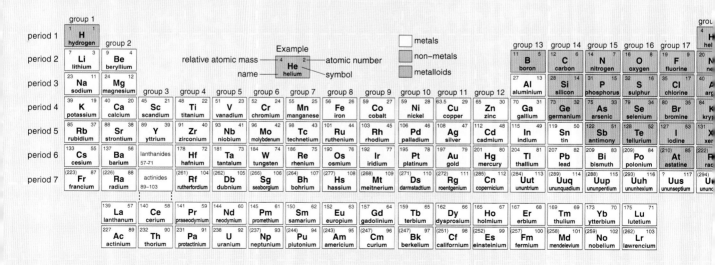

Sodium is a highly reactive metal. When a little water is dripped onto it, it explodes into sparks.

Missing pieces

Mendeleev's table had gaps in it. He knew there must be elements that hadn't been discovered. The patterns of atoms of different weights and properties showed that the missing atoms must exist, and the gaps would be filled as more elements were discovered. This did eventually happen.

"It is the function of science to discover the existence of a general reign of order in nature and to find the causes governing this order."

Dimitri Mendeleev describes his aim to discover an ordered pattern in the elements.

Secret structure

No one knew it at the time, but the periodic table actually gives a big insight into the structure of atoms. We now know that atoms are not whole, indivisible units, but are made up of much smaller **subatomic particles**. The way different atoms behave depends on how these particles are arranged. The periodic table helped scientists find out much more about this as time went on.

Breakthrough

Mendeleev's periodic table helped chemists understand the properties of different elements and their relationships with each other. It also helped them know what to look for when searching for new elements.

Radioactivity

The smallest unit?

All the previous advances revealed much more about matter and atoms than anyone had understood before. However, they still did not challenge the basic idea Democritus had come up with—that the atom was the smallest unit that existed, and it could not be divided. But this idea was about to be turned on its head with the discovery of **radioactivity**.

Becquerel's puzzle

In 1896, French scientist Henri Becquerel was experimenting with **X-rays**, a newly discovered form of energy. He wanted to know if

fluorescent crystals, which glow after absorbing light, gave out X-rays at the same time.

Becquerel set up an experiment to see if his crystals would make an X-ray image on a photographic plate. He expected it to work only after leaving the crystals in strong sunlight. However, he found that a

Marie Curie

Date of birth: November 7, 1867

Place of birth: Warsaw, Poland

Greatest achievement: Along with her husband, Pierre, and their colleague Henri Becquerel, Curie discovered and named radioactivity, and found out a lot about it.

Interesting fact: Marie Curie named the radioactive element polonium after her homeland, Poland.

Date of death: July 4, 1934

Radioactivity is very dangerous, but the Curies were not aware of this. Marie even slept with some glowing radium beside her bed because she thought it looked beautiful.

radioactivity from their atoms: **alpha particles**, **beta particles**, and **gamma rays**. Gamma rays are a type of energy wave, like light. But alpha and beta particles are actually parts of the atoms themselves, shooting out of them like tiny bullets. So atoms were not indivisible units after all.

mark appeared on the plate before this happened. The crystals were giving out another, unknown form of ray.

Radioactivity

Becquerel's colleagues, Marie and Pierre Curie, began studying the crystals he had used to see what was happening. They found that the mysterious rays were coming from one of the elements that made up the crystals—uranium. They did many other experiments and discovered other elements that did the same, such as radium and polonium.

Marie and Pierre Curie named this phenomenon "radioactivity," though at first they didn't know what caused it. Marie Curie continued to study it after Pierre died in 1906.

Bits of atoms

It eventually turned out that radioactive substances release three main types of

The three different types of radioactivity that can be emitted from radioactive atoms.

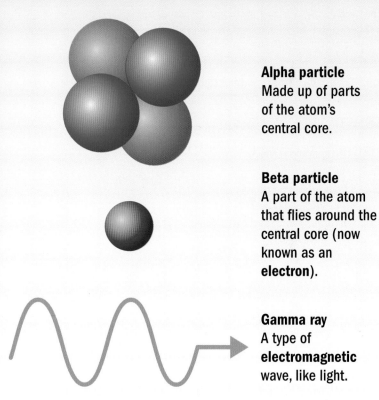

Alpha particle
Made up of parts of the atom's central core.

Beta particle
A part of the atom that flies around the central core (now known as an **electron**).

Gamma ray
A type of **electromagnetic** wave, like light.

Breakthrough

Thanks to the work of Henri Becquerel, Marie and Pierre Curie discovered radioactivity in the 1890s. This was a very important step in the journey toward splitting the atom.

The plum-pudding atom

Finding electrons

At the same time as radioactivity was being discovered, a completely different experiment also showed that atoms could come apart. In 1897, British scientist J. J. Thomson discovered the electron, one of the particles that makes up atoms.

Cathode rays

Thomson was experimenting with beams of electrical energy called **cathode rays**. They are made by running an electric circuit through a glass tube with all the air pumped out of it. One part of the circuit, the cathode, is at one end of the tube, and another, the anode, is at the other end, with a gap in the middle. When the electricity is switched on, a cathode ray streams across the gap.

Electron experiment

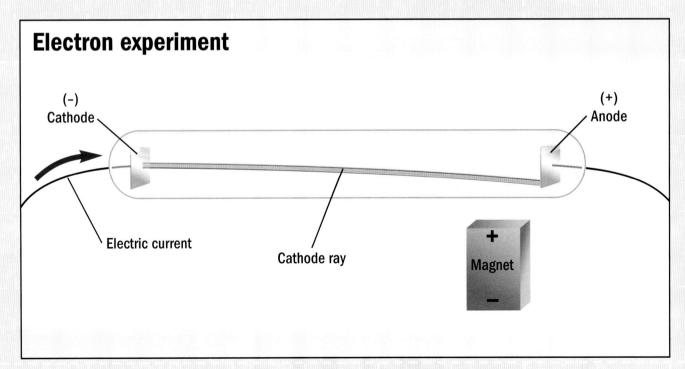

(–)
Cathode

(+)
Anode

Electric current

Cathode ray

+
Magnet
–

In this diagram, the thick line inside the tube is the cathode ray, a beam of electrons. Thomson found that the positive pole of a magnet could bend the ray toward it, showing that electrons had a negative charge.

No one knew what cathode rays were made of. Some said atoms, some said a type of light. So Thomson studied them closely and found that they were made of tiny particles, which had a negative electrical **charge**. He also found these particles were very light in weight—much lighter than the smallest atom. They were a new kind of particle, which he called corpuscles. Later, they were renamed electrons.

Breaking free

The electrons came from the metal cathode when electricity flowed through it. They were bits of its atoms that were breaking free and shooting across the gap between the cathode and the anode. That must mean that the metal's atoms contained many electrons.

Adding it up

Atoms don't normally have an electrical charge, but electrons do—they have a negative charge. Thomson thought that this meant an atom must contain something positively charged as well, so that the two forces would balance each other out. He decided that an atom might be like a "plum pudding"—a ball of positive electrical charge, filled with negatively-charged electrons, like plums evenly scattered through a cake. This was wrong, but it was one of the first attempts to construct a scientific model of what the inside of an atom looked like.

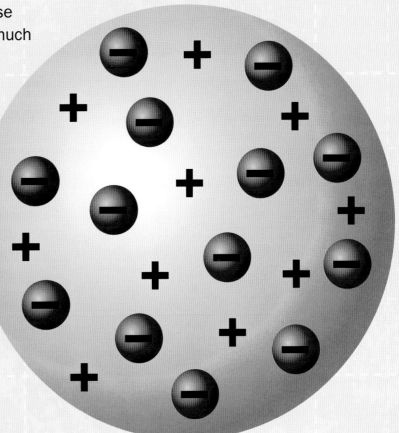

This diagram shows J. J. Thomson's "plum-pudding" model of the atom, with negatively-charged electrons scattered inside a positively-charged ball.

Breakthrough

J. J. Thomson was the first scientist to discover a subatomic particle—one of the minuscule particles that make up atoms. He was also the first to develop a theory about the structure of atoms. His work prompted other scientists to look inside an atom for the first time.

The gold foil experiment

Rutherford steps in

J. J. Thomson's model of the inside of an atom was sadly not quite correct. But it wasn't long before scientists would come up with a new, much more accurate description of atomic structure. The credit for this mostly goes to a great atomic scientist from New Zealand, Ernest Rutherford.

Mini bullets

In the early 1900s, scientists still weren't sure what the "alpha particles" that shot out of radioactive substances actually were. But they did know that they were solid, very small pieces of matter. They wondered what would happen if they used radioactive alpha particles as "bullets" to shoot at other atoms. Would this reveal something about how atoms were made?

In 1909, Rutherford and his colleagues, Hans Geiger and Ernest Marsden, were working in Manchester, England. They

The gold foil experiment was made up of just a few parts. The particle emitter shot alpha particles at a sheet of gold foil. A screen surrounding the foil detected where the particles ended up after hitting the foil.

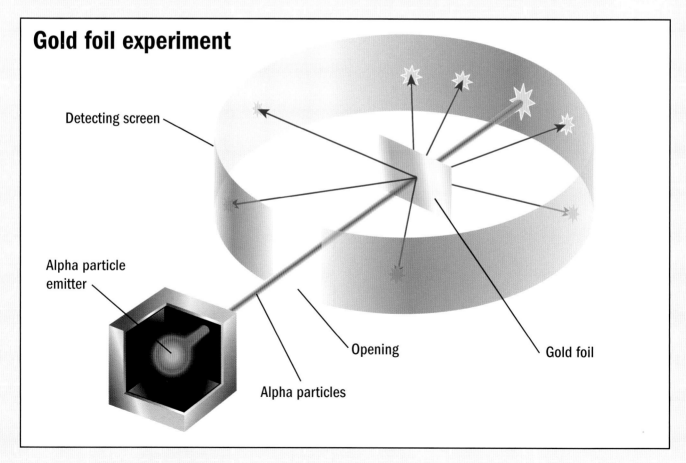

Gold foil experiment

Detecting screen

Alpha particle emitter

Alpha particles

Opening

Gold foil

came up with an experiment to fire alpha particles at a sheet of gold foil—which is made up of a very thin layer of millions of gold atoms. They could detect where the particles ended up afterward, by using a screen that showed a tiny flash when a particle hit it.

"It was the most incredible thing that has ever happened to me in my life. It was as if you fired a 15-inch (38-cm) shell [bullet] at a piece of tissue paper and it came back and hit you."
Ernest Rutherford describes his amazement at the results of the gold foil experiment.

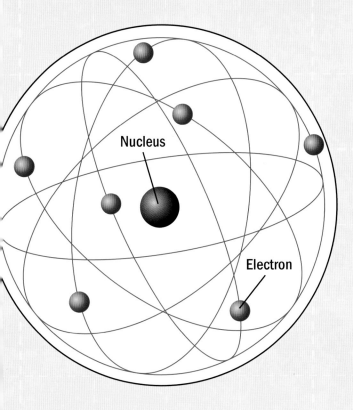

Nucleus

Electron

From his experiment, Rutherford came up with this new model of the atom. It had a heavy core or nucleus, with much smaller, lighter electrons zooming around it in a cloud.

Bouncing back

The results showed that most of the alpha particles shot straight through the foil and hit the screen. But occasionally, some were deflected sideways—and a few actually bounced back the way they had come.

Rutherford realized this meant the atom was not much like a plum pudding, as Thomson had thought. Instead it must have a tiny, solid, positively-charged core, or **nucleus**, surrounded by mostly empty space, with electrons floating around in it. When an alpha particle hit a gold atom, it usually flew freely through the empty part, or hit a lightweight electron that could not stop it. But sometimes it hit the hard, heavy nucleus and bounced off.

Breakthrough

Rutherford's gold foil experiment revealed that atoms are almost all empty space, with tiny electrons whizzing around a small solid core, or nucleus. He had conclusively proved the basic structure of atoms, which was a huge leap forward in atomic theory.

Electron shells

Improving the model

It wasn't long before Rutherford's atom model was improved upon yet again—by a Danish scientist named Niels Bohr, in 1913. Bohr's work gave us the model of the atom that scientists still use today.

Glowing with light

Bohr based his theory on a phenomenon called line spectra. When elements are heated, they give off light. Think of molten iron glowing red hot. When scientists studied this light, they found that each element only gives off light at particular energy levels. These levels can be shown as a range, or spectrum, of lines on a chart, and each element has its own unique "line spectrum."

When a blacksmith heats up iron to work with it, it glows first red, then yellow, and then white hot.

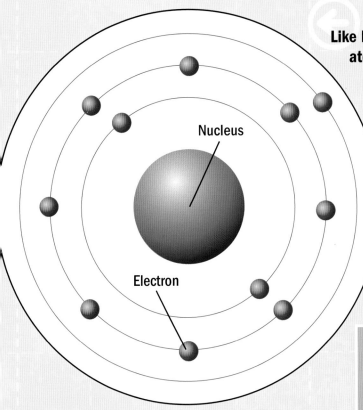

Nucleus

Electron

Like Rutherford's model, Bohr's "shell model" of the atom showed the electrons circling around the atom's nucleus—but in several separate energy levels, or "electron shells."

energy level, farther out. Then it would fall back down, and when this happened, the energy would be released as light—so energy went in as heat and came out as light. This explained why substances glowed when heated.

Niels Bohr said that this meant that when energy escaped from an atom, it escaped in "packets" or units, not as a continuous flow. To explain this, he said that an atom's electrons did not zoom randomly all around it. Instead, they were trapped in separate energy layers, or "**electron shells**," around the atom's nucleus.

How it works

Bohr said that when energy was added to an atom, for example by heating it, an electron could jump from a lower-energy level, close to the nucleus, to a higher-

"Anyone who is not shocked by quantum theory has not understood it."
This quotation from Niels Bohr shows that he knew just how strange quantum theory was.

Quantum theory

Bohr was a leader in the development of the strange field of **quantum theory**. According to quantum principles, tiny particles can behave in ways that are impossible in our everyday experience. For example, when electrons jump or leap between shells, Bohr said, they did not travel between them—they just disappeared from one and instantly appeared in the other. Quantum experiments have also shown that a single electron can be in two places at once. Quantum science is very hard to understand, and scientists are still trying to unravel it.

Breakthrough

Bohr's shell model was a huge step in chemistry. It defined the structure of the atom and helped explain chemical reactions. The number of electrons in an atom's outer shell decides how that atom joins to other atoms to make molecules.

Going deeper

It was known that atoms had two main parts—a nucleus in the middle, and an outer area where electrons zoomed around. But what was the nucleus made of? It took a while to discover the two particles that make up an atomic nucleus—**protons** and **neutrons**.

Protons

The key to the discovery of protons was the element hydrogen. It is the smallest and lightest type of atom, as it has just

one electron and its nucleus is made of just one proton. In 1919, Ernest Rutherford tried directing alpha particles emitted by radioactive materials into nitrogen gas. When an alpha particle hit

James Chadwick built this device in 1932 to detect neutrons being given off by some types of radioactive materials.

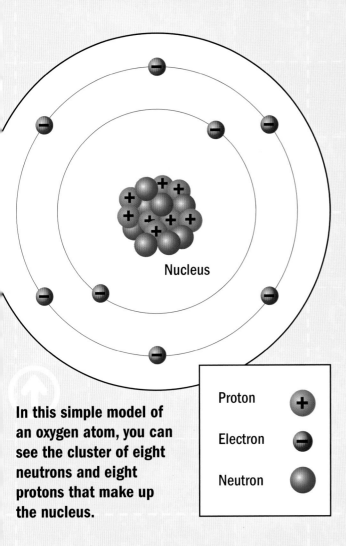

In this simple model of an oxygen atom, you can see the cluster of eight neutrons and eight protons that make up the nucleus.

Proton	+
Electron	−
Neutron	

a nitrogen nucleus, something that behaved like a hydrogen atom without its electron was knocked out of it. Rutherford named this unit the proton.

Neutrons

Scientists thought that another atomic particle must exist, but they couldn't detect it. Then, in 1930, they found that firing alpha particles at the element beryllium made a new kind of radioactive energy shoot out. In 1932, a British scientist named James Chadwick found that this **radiation** was made of particles that had no electrical

Isotopes

In 1913, British chemist Frederick Soddy found that atoms of the same element are actually not all identical, as they can have different weights. These different forms of the same atom were named "isotopes" by Soddy's cousin, Dr. Margaret Todd. Scientists later found that different isotopes of an atom have different numbers of neutrons. So, for example, oxygen normally has 8 neutrons, but some oxygen atoms have 9 or 10.

charge, but were similar in size to protons. They were named neutrons.

Doing the math

Now scientists knew that atoms contained negatively-charged electrons, positively-charged protons, and neutral neutrons. They also knew the weight of each type of element. Each atom had to have a certain number of each particle to make it the right weight and to make its charges cancel each other out. This meant they could now calculate what each type of atom was made of. For example, we now know that an oxygen atom has 8 protons, 8 neutrons, and 8 electrons.

Breakthrough

The discovery of protons and neutrons in the first half of the 20th century finally solved the question of how atoms were constructed.

Could the atom be split?

Rutherford leads the way

In one sense, it was clear that atoms could be split apart. Electrons separated from their atoms in a cathode ray tube, and radioactive atoms shot out some of their particles. But could scientists break an atomic nucleus apart deliberately? And what would happen if they did? Once again, Ernest Rutherford led the research.

Changing the atom

Around 1917–9, Rutherford tried a series of experiments to try to "disintegrate," or chip away at, atomic nuclei. He used radioactive substances such as radium to provide a stream of alpha particles, which he shot at different elements. In 1919, he had an amazing success with nitrogen gas. He made the alpha particles enter the nitrogen nucleus. An alpha particle is actually made of two protons and two neutrons. They combined with the nitrogen nucleus and a proton flew out. The nitrogen atom was turned into two other types of atom: an oxygen atom and a hydrogen atom.

Ernest Rutherford

Date of birth: August 30, 1871

Place of birth: Nelson, New Zealand

Greatest achievement:
Rutherford was the true father of nuclear science. He discovered the basic structure of the atom, and the proton. His experiments laid the groundwork for splitting the atom and all the incredible consequences that followed.

Interesting fact: Whenever one of his experiments went well, Rutherford would loudly sing his favorite hymn, "Onward Christian Soldiers."

Date of death: October 19, 1937

Rutherford's transmutation experiment

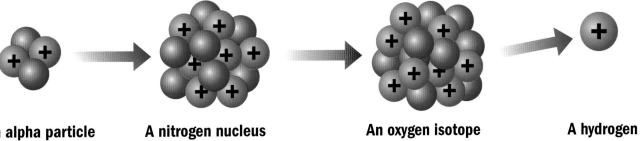

An alpha particle
(2 protons,
2 neutrons—
a helium nucleus)

A nitrogen nucleus
(7 protons, 7 neutrons)

**An oxygen isotope
nucleus**
(8 protons, 9 neutrons)

**A hydrogen
nucleus**
(1 proton)

Alchemy at last

What Rutherford had done was what alchemists hundreds of years ago had tried to achieve. He had turned one element into another. This is called "transmutation," and it was the first time it had ever been done deliberately. But it wasn't really splitting the atom. Instead, he had just added three nuclear particles to a nitrogen atom to make oxygen. The remaining proton that shot out was hydrogen.

Natural transmutation

Transmutation of atoms also happens in nature, in radioactive substances. As they give out alpha particles, their nuclei change and they become other, less radioactive elements. For example, when a uranium atom emits an alpha particle, it becomes thorium. When a plutonium atom emits an alpha particle, it becomes uranium.

This diagram shows what happened in Rutherford's 1919 transmutation experiment. An alpha particle (or helium nucleus) containing two protons and two neutrons smashed into a nitrogen nucleus, building it up into an oxygen nucleus instead. One spare proton shot out, forming a hydrogen atom.

More power

The alpha particles Rutherford used moved quite fast but not quickly enough to be really powerful. Rutherford saw that, to try and smash atomic nuclei apart, he needed a way of making alpha particles go faster.

Breakthrough

Rutherford's 1919 transmutation of the atom was a huge breakthrough. It showed that nuclear particles fired from outside an atom could enter and change its nucleus. So what next? Could the atom actually be split?

The particle accelerator

Speeding up

To make particles move faster than they would naturally, scientists realized that they could use a powerful **electric field**. If it was set up in the right way, it could pull on particles, controlling their direction and making them speed up.

Making an accelerator

Previously, it had been difficult to create an electrical field that was strong enough. But in the 1920s, new technology made this possible. Rutherford was now head of the Cavendish Laboratory in Cambridge, England. Two of his colleagues there, John Cockroft and Ernest Walton, began experimenting with different designs for

"It is not the nature of things for any one man to make a sudden, violent discovery; science goes step by step and every man depends on the work of his predecessors."
Rutherford describing the process of science. This was very true of Cockroft and Walton's work on splitting the atom, which built on Rutherford's own discoveries.

THAT'S A FACT!

The world's biggest particle accelerator is the Large Hadron Collider. This huge underground ring is 6 miles (9 km) across (see pages 40–41).

a "particle accelerator" to speed up, or accelerate, subatomic particles.

Eventually, around 1930, they developed the first working model. It used 100,000 volts of electricity to fire protons at high speed along a straight tube, to be used as bullets for firing at other atoms.

Round in a ring

At the same time, an American team, Ernest Lawrence and Stanley Livingstone, were building another type of accelerator. It worked by making particles speed up as they whizzed around inside a ring-shaped tube. This model is still used for some of the biggest particle accelerators today.

What kind of particles?

Many of Rutherford's great experiments had involved firing alpha particles at atoms. An alpha particle, given out by some radioactive substances, is a small cluster of two neutrons and two protons. It is quite heavy and is therefore good at breaking through other substances, as in Rutherford's gold foil experiment. But as time went on, scientists tried using much smaller, single atomic particles instead—one proton or one neutron at a time. This gave different kinds of results and allowed for more experiments.

Cockroft and Walton's 1932 particle accelerator at the Cavendish Laboratory in Cambridge, England. You can see John Cockroft himself sitting under part of the generator.

Breakthrough

The invention of the particle accelerator opened up new possibilities in atomic science. As well as contributing to the splitting of the atom, it helped scientists find out much more about the particles of which matter is made.

Splitting the atom

The breakthrough

It's hard to pick one moment that counts as the very first splitting of the atom, as it depends on how you define it. It was really a gradual process, with different scientists dismantling and altering atoms in various ways over the years. However, many experts agree that the most important breakthrough came in 1932.

Splitting lithium in two

On April 14 of that year, Cockroft and Walton tried out their new particle accelerator under controlled laboratory conditions. They used it to shoot high-speed protons at atoms of lithium, a metallic element. They could detect the

"Splitting the atom is like trying to shoot a gnat in the Albert Hall at night."
Ernest Rutherford describes how tricky it is to find the nucleus of an atom. The Albert Hall is a large concert hall in London.

Ernest Rutherford (center) with Ernest Walton (left) and John Cockroft (right), photographed in 1932 after the successful atom-splitting experiment was announced.

results of their experiment using a detecting screen that flashed in different ways when each type of particle hit it.

The scientists didn't expect any astounding results on their first try, but looking at their detecting screen, they were amazed to see flashes that they recognized as alpha particles. But they had not fired any alpha particles in—just protons. What was happening?

How it worked

The lithium atoms in the experiment each had a nucleus containing three protons and four neutrons.

1.
High-speed protons were fired at the lithium atoms.

2.
When the speeding proton hit the nucleus, it split the lithium atom, making a total of four protons and four neutrons.

3.
They reformed into two clusters, each containing two neutrons and two protons—in other words, two alpha particles. The nucleus had been split right in two.

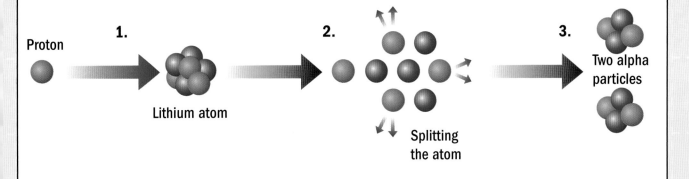

Proton

1.

Lithium atom

2.

Splitting the atom

3.

Two alpha particles

THAT'S A FACT!

Cockroft and Walton used a children's modeling clay, called plasticine, to seal the gaps in their particle accelerator during their famous 1932 experiment.

Breakthrough

Cockroft and Walton's key 1932 experiment led to the first controlled, artificial complete splitting of the atom into two parts. Though later experiments would do things differently, successfully splitting the atom paved the way for a series of astounding inventions that would change the world.

More experimentation

Now everyone knew that splitting the atom was possible, other scientists made their own particle accelerators and tried out more and more atom-splitting experiments. This led to a great discovery. Splitting the atom released energy.

Neutron bullets

Many scientists switched to using neutrons as "bullets." Unlike protons and alpha particles, they were neutral, with no electrical charge. Opposite charges attract each other, and alike charges repel each other. But neutral neutrons were not affected by the atom's own charged particles and could enter an atom's nucleus more easily.

Splitting radioactive atoms

In the mid-1930s, some scientists, such as Italian Enrico Fermi and Austrian-born Lise Meitner, tried atom-splitting experiments with atoms of radioactive elements. When they fired neutrons into a radioactive atom's nucleus, it would split easily and form new, different types of radioactive atoms. This method would eventually become very important.

Extra energy

During this work, scientists uncovered an amazing fact. When an atom split, the mass (amount of matter) in the particles after the experiment was slightly reduced. Meanwhile, a lot of energy was released. As the newly-split particles shot away from the nucleus, they moved with incredible speed, far greater than the force that had been used to fire particles in.

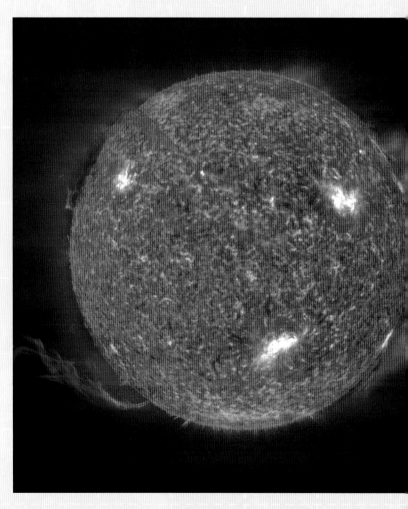

Matter is converted into energy inside the sun, as the result of a process called nuclear fission.

Some of the many scientists involved in developing atom-splitting methods in the 1930s. They include Ernest Rutherford (seated center), James Chadwick (seated far left), and Lise Meitner and Otto Hahn (standing either side of Rutherford).

The scientists realized that they had proved a famous theory proposed in 1905 by the great German scientist Albert Einstein. Einstein's theory had a simple formula: $E=mc^2$. This meant that mass (m) could turn into energy (E). When this happened, it only took a tiny amount of mass to make a lot of energy. And splitting an atom could release it.

Einstein's theory

This is what Einstein's theory $E=mc^2$ actually means.

E is energy
m is mass
c is the speed of light

If a given amount of matter is turned into energy, the amount of energy released is equivalent to the amount of matter multiplied by the speed of light squared. The speed of light is a very big number, and when squared (multiplied by itself) it's even bigger. So, in other words, a very small amount of matter converts into a huge amount of energy.

New energy source?

The discovery that splitting the atom converted matter into energy was very important. It meant that, perhaps, splitting atoms could become a source of energy that humans could use. And if so, in what ways would it be used? Ernest Rutherford did not believe it would happen. He was wrong, but perhaps he simply didn't want to think about the frightening possibilities.

Breakthrough

Scientists discovered that splitting the atom converted matter into energy. This confirmed Einstein's theory and opened up exciting and frightening possibilities.

The atomic bomb

An atomic explosion?

The scientists who split the atom just wanted to find out more about atoms and how they worked. They had no bad intentions. Like most scientists, when they discovered something new and exciting, they wanted to find out more about it. But it wasn't long before some began to wonder if the energy released by splitting the atom could be used to make a huge, powerful explosion—an atomic bomb. Many scientists were worried about this.

> *"You must not blame us scientists for the use to which war technicians have put our discoveries."*
> Atomic scientist Lise Meitner on the invention of the atomic bomb, on which she herself refused to work.

War breaks out

As the 1930s reached their end, German leader Adolf Hitler began to invade other European countries and war was declared in 1939—World War II had begun.

The issue of an atomic bomb suddenly became urgent. Some of the scientists who had been working on atomic science were German, or living in Germany. Many fled abroad, but others stayed and worked for the German side. They included the quantum scientist Werner Heisenberg, a former colleague and friend of Niels Bohr. If the Germans were going to make an atomic bomb, the other side, known as the Allied Nations, wanted to beat them to it.

This picture shows the huge, high mushroom cloud that developed when an atomic bomb was dropped on Nagasaki in Japan in 1945.

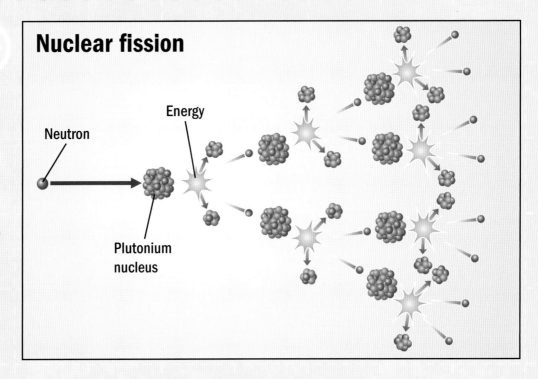

Nuclear fission

Neutron

Energy

Plutonium
nucleus

This diagram shows a nuclear fission chain reaction. As one atom is split, it releases particles that go on to split other nearby atoms, and the explosion grows at a rapid rate.

Make it now!

The United States of America, one of the Allied Nations, set up a project called the Manhattan Project, directed by a scientist named Robert Oppenheimer, to make an atomic bomb as soon as possible. They asked scientists from all over Europe to go to the United States to help. As a result, Enrico Fermi, and two scientists who had escaped from Germany, Otto Frisch and Rudolf Peierls, found a way to make an atom-splitting chain reaction using radioactive elements. Splitting one atomic nucleus of uranium or plutonium released particles that then went on to split other nearby atoms, in a runaway chain reaction that caused a massive explosion.

This process was perfected by 1942, and three years later, the first atomic bombs were actually used in warfare. The Americans dropped them on the Japanese cities of Hiroshima and Nagasaki in 1945 to force the Japanese, who were on the German side, to surrender. These bombings ended the war but also killed many thousands of innocent people and shocked the world.

Was it wrong?

Why did some scientists agree to work on a deadly atomic bomb? Although many of them felt terrible about it, scientists on both sides thought they were working for a good cause. But it came at a terrible cost.

Breakthrough

The invention of the atomic bomb in the early 1940s unleashed a terrifying weapon of previously unseen power.

Nuclear power

Making electricity

The atomic bomb was a deadly and frightening consequence of advances in splitting the atom. But there was a more positive side to the discovery. After World War II was over, scientists began working on ways to use a nuclear chain reaction to make a gentler, more controlled supply of energy. Instead of a sudden explosion, this slower process releases heat that can be used to run power plants for generating electricity. The first nuclear power plant opened in Russia in 1954, and, since then, hundreds more have been built in many parts of the world.

THAT'S A FACT!

Radioactive waste from nuclear power plants continues to be hazardous for over 200,000 years.

Is it clean?

Nuclear power produces electricity without releasing polluting waste gases into the air, as happens when burning fossil fuels

This nuclear power plant in Lianyungang is one of eastern China's key energy providers.

Why is it dangerous?

Radioactivity is harmful to humans because radioactive particles and rays carry a lot of energy. When they hit our bodies, they enter our **cells** and damage or change the molecules there, including DNA (the molecule that makes our genes). This can make the chemical balance inside a cell change, so that it doesn't work properly. Or it can force cells to multiply too quickly, causing **cancer**.

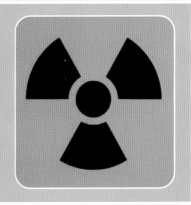

In Belarus, people wear masks during a rally on April 26, 2008. The rally marked the 22nd anniversary of the Chernobyl's tragedy.

1986, an accident at the Chernobyl Nuclear Power Plant in the USSR (now part of the Ukraine) caused an atomic explosion that released a huge cloud of radioactive material. Forty-seven workers were killed, and it's thought that thousands more people died in the following years from diseases caused by the radiation. More than 300,000 people had to be evacuated from their homes.

such as coal and gas. However, it has downsides, too. Nuclear power plants create a small amount of harmful radioactive waste, which has to be stored safely so that radioactive particles cannot leak from it. However, doing this still causes problems as the storage methods are not always very effective, and the waste can sometimes leak.

There have also been accidents at nuclear power plants that have released dangerous radiation over a large area. In

Breakthrough

Nuclear power—splitting the atom to provide an energy supply—gave us a new way to generate electricity. It has now been used for more than 50 years.

Back to the lab

Splitting the atom was a turning point in the history of the world. But it was far from being the end of the study of atoms. After World War II ended in 1945, scientists were free to turn back to the pure scientific study of atoms. And now that governments were not spending so much money on weapons, they could afford to fund new equipment and research. In the 1950s, new, more powerful particle accelerators were developed to smash atoms and particles together at even greater speeds.

Bubble chambers

In 1952, a U.S. scientist, Donald A Glaser, invented the bubble chamber. This device can reveal the movements of tiny subatomic particles in amazing detail. It is a tank filled with liquid, such as liquid hydrogen, at a particular pressure and **density**. As particles move in the liquid, they create a trail of tiny bubbles. The bubbles grow bigger and become visible, making the particle tracks clear enough to be recorded on camera. The bubble chamber has now been replaced by newer methods, but it allowed many new discoveries.

Even smaller particles

Using this new technology, scientists found that atoms were even more complex than they had thought. Subatomic particles such as protons and neutrons were made up of even tinier "elementary

This massive piece of equipment is the magnet core of the Large Hadron Collider, being put into place during the Collider's assembly in 2007.

particles," named quarks and leptons. Each of these is divided into six different types, depending on their charge and other properties. This theory of elementary particles is known as the Standard Model.

New experiments

Scientists are still carrying out experiments on atoms today to try to find out more about how matter works. Massive particle accelerators, such as the Large Hadron Collider, are designed to carry out experiments that may answer many of their questions.

The Large Hadron Collider is the newest and biggest particle accelerator to be built. The ring on this landscape shows where it lies more than 328 feet (100 m) underground near Geneva in Switzerland.

The Higgs boson

The Higgs boson is a mysterious "missing" elementary particle. The Standard Model says that it must exist in order to explain why matter has mass, but it has not been found anywhere. Scientists are hoping to discover it by using a particle accelerator to create conditions like those that existed at the time of the **Big Bang**, at the start of the universe. They hope this will result in Higgs boson particles existing for a short time. The Higgs boson got its name from Peter Higgs, one of several scientists who predicted its existence in 1964.

"I'll be very surprised if they don't find it [the Higgs boson]."
Peter Higgs, speaking in 2008, expresses his confidence that the Higgs boson will soon be discovered.

Breakthrough

The Standard Model of elementary particles that make up matter was developed and perfected between about 1960 and 1967. It provides a basic theory of matter that is still in use today.

Atomic mysteries

The nature of matter

All these discoveries, while revealing more and more about atoms and the particles they are made of, have still not solved a great mystery—the true nature of matter. What is all the "stuff" that makes up our universe? However small you go, and however tiny the particles you discover, there is always another question: what are those particles made of?

The big question

The answer is that, despite years of amazing advances, no one is really sure. Scientists have come up with many theories to explain what matter actually is and how it works. But these ideas are incredibly complicated and hard to prove. They are trying to describe

things on an unimaginably tiny scale—and that makes it hard to see what is really happening. And, as quantum theory shows, on a tiny scale, matter doesn't always behave in the ways we expect.

Leading physicist Stephen Hawking presenting some of his work on how the universe, and the matter it is made of, might have come into existence.

Weirder and weirder

In fact, the more you think about matter, the stranger it seems. Our planet, cities homes, furniture, food, computers, books, toys, ourselves, and all other living things, are mainly empty space. What is there is still something of a mystery to science. We have only just scratched the surface of how matter works and where it came from.

Perhaps, if you become a particle physicist, you could become one of the future scientists who can shed more light on this perplexing puzzle.

String theory

"String theory" is a name given to one of the leading ideas about how matter works. It also explains gravity and other forces, all bound together by one theory—known as the "theory of everything." It gets its name because it originally described reality as a system of tiny vibrating stringlike shapes—although it can be seen as single points or surfaces instead, so the name "string" is not really accurate. Scientists are still working on various types of string theory, as well as other ideas. One day, they may be able to develop this into a clearer idea of how reality works.

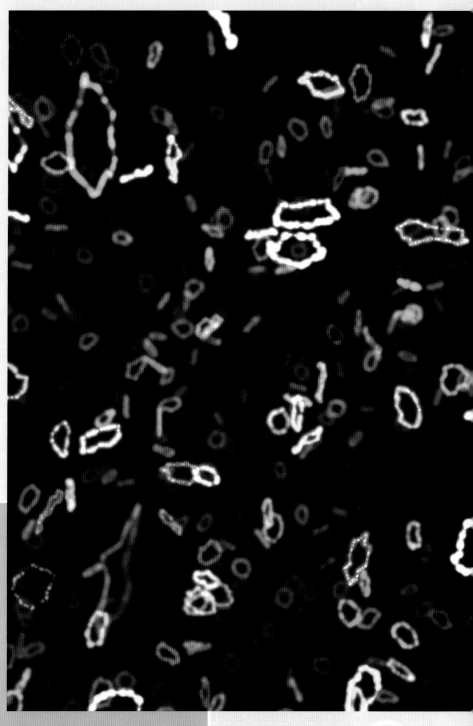

This is a computer-generated image attempting to visualize string theory—but as the theory involves more than three dimensions, it is very hard to show in a picture.

Glossary

alpha particle a type of radiation given off by some radioactive substances. Alpha particles are each made up of two protons and two neutrons.

atom one of the tiny units of which matter is made

beta particles a type of radiation given off by some radioactive substances

Big Bang the massive explosion that many people believe marked the birth of our universe, firing matter in all directions

Buddhist a follower of Buddhism, a religion that began in India

cancer a medical condition caused by abnormal cell growth that causes tumors

cathode ray a beam of electrons that travel along a cathode ray tube

cathode ray tube a vacuum-filled glass tube forming part of an electric circuit

cell one of the tiny "building blocks" that make up all living things

charge an electrical property of matter that can be either negative or positive—for example, in atomic science, electrons have a negative charge, and protons have a positive charge

chemical reaction a process in which a chemical substance or substances change into different substances by rearranging their atoms and molecules

compound a substance made up of two or more different types of atoms bonded or joined together in molecules

density a measure of how much matter a material or object contains compared to its volume

electric field an area of space influenced by an electrical charge

electromagnetic something that consists of both electric and magnetic components

electron a very small subatomic particle that moves around the nucleus inside an atom

electron shell one of the energy levels or layers around the nucleus of an atom in which electrons can orbit the nucleus

element a basic form of matter made up of just one type of atom

energy a force that causes motion, movement, or power

gamma rays a type of radiation given off by some radioactive substances. Gamma rays are a form of energy wave, like light and X-rays.

matter the three-dimensional, real stuff that makes up the universe

medieval a period in European history, from approximately A.D. 500 to the 1400s

molecule the smallest part of an element or compound that can exist, made up of two or more atoms bonded together

neutron one of the subatomic particles that make up the nucleus of an atom

nucleus (plural: nuclei) the core or middle part of an atom

philosopher someone who thinks and has ideas about how the world works

physicist a scientist who studies physics, the science of matter and energy

properties the features and qualities of a particular element or other substance, and the way it behaves

proton one of the subatomic particles that make up the nucleus of an atom

quantum theory a branch of scientific theory dealing with some aspects of the behavior of particles of matter and energy waves

radiation a name for the rays or particles given off by radioactive substances

radioactivity a feature of some elements that means they give out beams of subatomic particles or energy rays

react when a substance reacts with another, it means that a chemical change takes place because the two substances have been put together

Renaissance a period of great cultural change in European history, dating from the 1400s to the 1700s

subatomic particle one of the tiny particles of which atoms are made

X-rays a type of energy wave similar to light

Further information

Books

Albert Einstein: Genius of the Twentieth Century by Allison Lassieur. Children's Press, 2005.

Atom by Piers Bizony. Icon Books, 2008.

Exploring Atoms and Molecules by Nigel Saunders. Rosen Publishing Group, 2007.

Splitting the Atom by Alan Morton. Evans Brothers, 2008.

What Do You Think? Is Nuclear Power Safe? by John Meany. Heinemann Library, 2008.

Some useful web sites

The Discovery of Radioactivity: The Dawn of the Nuclear Age
www.accessexcellence.org/AE/AEC/CC/radioactivity.php
Facts about the discovery of radioactivity, with links to information about the scientists involved.

Basic Nuclear Fission
library.thinkquest.org/17940
This web site examines nuclear processes including what happens when an atom is split.

Einstein's Big Idea
www.pbs.org/wgbh/nova/einstein
Everything you could want to know about Albert Einstein and his groundbreaking theory, $E=mc^2$.

History of Energy
tonto.eia.doe.gov/kids/energy.cfm?page=4
Contains useful information about nuclear power and some of the scientists involved in splitting the atom.

How Stuff Works
www.howstuffworks.com/atom.html
Another site with animations about atoms and how they split.

Index